SC1

2008

7/09 · 2/10

x 5/10 10/11

The Myth of Multitasking

How "Doing It All" Gets Nothing Done

Dave Crenshaw

JOSSEY-BASS
A Wiley Imprint
www.josseybass.com

Published by Jossey-Bass
A Wiley Imprint
989 Market Street, San Francisco, CA 94103–1741—www.josseybass.com

Readers should be aware that Internet Web sites offered as citations and/or sources for further information may have changed or disappeared between the time this was written and when it is read.

Limit of Liability/Disclaimer of Warranty: While the publisher and author have used their best efforts in preparing this book, they make no representations or warranties with respect to the accuracy or completeness of the contents of this book and specifically disclaim any implied warranties of merchantability or fitness for a particular purpose. No warranty may be created or extended by sales representatives or written sales materials. The advice and strategies contained herein may not be suitable for your situation. You should consult with a professional where appropriate. Neither the publisher nor author shall be liable for any loss of profit or any other commercial damages, including but not limited to special, incidental, consequential, or other damages.

Jossey-Bass books and products are available through most bookstores. To contact Jossey-Bass directly call our Customer Care Department within the U.S. at 800–956–7739, outside the U.S. at 317–572–3986, or fax 317–572–4002.

Jossey-Bass also publishes its books in a variety of electronic formats. Some content that appears in print may not be available in electronic books.

Library of Congress Cataloging-in-Publication Data

Crenshaw, Dave, 1975-
    The myth of multitasking : how "doing it all" gets nothing done / Dave Crenshaw.
        p.   cm.—(The Jossey-Bass business & management series)
    Includes index.
    ISBN 978-0-470-37225-8 (cloth)
        1. Time management.   2. Executives—Time management.
    3. Organizational change.   4. Management.   I. Title.
    HD69.T54C74   2008
    658.4'093—dc22
                                                                    2008014797

Printed in the United States of America
FIRST EDITION

HB Printing   10 9 8 7 6 5 4 3 2 1

CONTENTS

Contents

For Carlos,
who always taught me to
"move very slowly, but in a great rush"

THE COMPANY

Phil glanced at the digital clock on his sedan. It read 8:54 A.M. He nodded to himself in satisfaction at being several minutes early. He had learned years ago that if he was going to teach efficiency and time management to others, he had better be living it himself.

After grabbing his briefcase, Phil opened his car door and stepped out. He turned and looked up at the sign on the sprawling building that proudly proclaimed GreenGarb: Clothes Mother Nature Intended.

Phil had done his research about his new coaching client. Helen Whitman had been an influential executive in a large retail clothing chain for nearly a decade. Just a few years ago, however, she recognized the trend toward eco-friendly products and decided

1

to make the jump into entrepreneurship. Last year, GreenGarb boasted sales of over $20 million and was heading for even greater growth.

Despite the success—or more likely because of it—Helen had hit a brick wall. After a bit of burnout, Helen had contacted a few close friends, asking for a referral to someone who could help.

As Phil walked toward the building, he reflected on his first conversation with Helen. Her situation was all too familiar. While the company sizes and industries of Phil's clients varied greatly, their stories were echoes of each other. His clients were stressed out, overworked, and underpaid. They were finding themselves with more and more to do at work and less and less time for their family and other personal life.

These business owners all came to Phil for help. They were looking for someone who understood that it was lonely at the top. They were looking for someone who could help them make the behavior corrections that would get them more time and less stress.

Helen's company was unique, but her story was the same.

As he walked through the front door of the building, Phil was greeted by a receptionist with a no-nonsense look about her. Phil found his mouth a little dry as he spoke up.

"I'm here to see Helen."

The receptionist looked up. "Do you have an appointment?"

"Yes. Yes, I do."

"Just a moment." The receptionist pressed the intercom button and politely said, "Ms. Whitman? There is a gentleman here at the front who says he has an appointment with you." After listening to the response, she said, "Please follow me."

As Phil followed the receptionist down the hall, he glanced in each direction and noticed the offices of the company managers. There was a general feeling of controlled chaos on all sides. A few desks appeared organized, but most offices had piles of papers on the desk that occasionally flowed onto the floor. People walked in and out of the offices in a hurry, speaking in brisk, determined tones to each other.

Phil had certainly seen this before. Just by looking into the offices of the company managers, Phil grew a bit more comfortable. He knew what to expect when he walked into Helen's office. In fact, he knew what to expect from Helen. The common saying was true: the business truly is a reflection of its owner.

THE OWNER

The situation in the CEO's office was just short of chaos. A woman with glasses shot him a glance as if to say, "If you're here for Helen, wait in line." Phil smiled. Helen waved Phil in and gestured to an open chair. "Please, come in and have a seat. We're just finishing up."

Phil moved to the chair and considered the scene carefully. Two men whom Phil guessed were managers were sitting at the small conference table with Helen.

The woman with glasses stood impatiently, watching the proceedings. It was obvious to Phil she was not part of the conversation and was eager for a moment to catch Helen's ear. Phil watched her with curiosity. She was biting her lower lip just slightly, trying to contain herself.

Finally the managers completed their conversation with Helen and stood up from the table.

Helen turned to the woman, displaying a bit of her own impatience. "Yes, Sally, what is it?" As Sally began speaking, Helen turned to Phil and interjected, "This will take just a moment, I'm sorry."

Sally sighed audibly.

"No need to be sorry," Phil replied. He could sense the tension in the room and was doing his best to diffuse it. Helen turned back to Sally and shot a controlled, "Go."

"I wish we could have talked about this before you went into that meeting. I have a supplier in Kansas who is chomping at the bit. He wants to know if you approved the change in color from khaki to light tan."

Now Helen bit her bottom lip. She was clearly attempting to control her emotions. "Sally, I talked to him yesterday and told him everything he needed to know."

"So what is the answer?"

"Tell him *again* that light tan is fine. Delaying our shipment is not!"

"Got it. Um . . ." Sally stood motionless in front of Helen. Phil could tell she was going through her memory to find something to tell Helen.

"Yes?"

Sudden recognition flashed across Sally's face. "Did you get to the designs I sent to you yesterday?"

Helen sighed. "No, Sally. I haven't. I've been buried. I'm trying to do a million things. I'll get to it sometime today."

Sally shrugged. "Fine." She turned and left abruptly.

"Sally?" Helen called out.

"Yes?" Sally said, turning. She was obviously anticipating something of great importance.

"Please close the door behind you."

THE LIE

Helen began speaking in a rush. "Phil, I just don't have enough time to do everything I need to! Everyone is constantly demanding my attention. I'm behind on checking my e-mail. My voice mail is full. I'm constantly thinking about what I need to do! Helen shook her head as her voice trailed off. "I guess that's what you're here for, isn't it?"

"Yes," said Phil sympathetically, and glanced around the room. "So, just to check in regarding the phone conversation we had last week, have you been able to let everyone know that we're going to be meeting today? Will we be able to have uninterrupted time?"

"I guess so," Helen sighed. "I've told everybody that I was not to be disturbed. However, there is one call I need to take if it comes in."

Phil smiled. "Okay, then." He leaned forward in his chair and looked her directly in the eyes. "Tell me, Helen: When I say the word *multitasking,* what comes to mind?"

Helen's face changed into a broad smile of self-satisfaction. "Me," she said.

"You? What do you mean?"

"Me! I'm an excellent multitasker. I'm the Queen of Multitasking. It's actually a requirement when we post ads for new hires. My employees are all expected to be good multitaskers."

Phil grinned and leaned back in his chair. "Then you may be shocked with what I'm about to teach you." He paused. "Do you like Mark Twain?"

Helen looked puzzled. "Sure, I like Mark Twain. I read *Huckleberry Finn* when I was in high school. What does he have to do with multitasking?" Phil rocked his head casually from side to side. "Actually, not much. Mark Twain was credited with a quote— maybe you've heard it: 'There are lies, damned lies, and statistics.'"

Helen chuckled softly. "I've heard that before."

"Let me give you a different version, a twenty-first-century version. It goes like this: 'There are lies, damned lies, and multitasking.'" Phil stopped and waited for a reaction.

Helen blinked. "I don't get it. Why is multitasking a lie?"

"It isn't a lie," Phil smiled. "It's worse than a lie. It's even worse than a damned lie."

"Why do you say that?"

"It's a lie because nearly everyone in our fast-paced world has accepted it as something that's true. We've all adopted it as a way of life. People are proud of their skills at multitasking, but the truth is that multitasking is neither a reality nor is it efficient."

Helen scowled just slightly. "I don't think I understand. I'm constantly doing more than one thing at a time. I make use of every spare minute I have. I get more done than most anyone I know." She tapped her pen on the desk and threw a challenging look at Phil.

Phil nodded. "I don't doubt you're a hard worker. Maybe you're the hardest worker I've ever met. Yet are you getting the results you want?"

Helen sighed. "Obviously not. Otherwise I wouldn't have hired you to help me, but I thought you were going to help me be more efficient and effective. I didn't know you were going to talk to me about multitasking."

"Your lack of effectiveness has everything to do with your multitasking."

THE COST

Phil paused and pulled out a notepad. "I'm going to explain to you why multitasking is worse than a lie. First, do you mind if I ask you a few questions and take some notes?"

"Sure. Fire away."

"How many e-mails do you get per day?" Phil asked.

"Way too many," Helen muttered. She thought for a moment. "I probably have over forty in there, and it's only nine o'clock in the morning!"

Phil jotted a note down. "And realistically speaking, how many times a day do you check your e-mail?"

Helen shrugged. "I need to stay on top of things, or I'll get buried. I guess I check it every hour or so."

She snapped her fingers suddenly. "Wait! My phone is set to receive e-mail too. I'd be lost without that! Do you want me to include checking e-mail on my phone?"

Phil nodded silently.

"Okay. I probably check my e-mail a couple of times per hour then," Helen said.

Phil marked Helen's response in his notebook. "Okay. How many times are you interrupted by coworkers during the day?"

"Too many times to count," Helen groaned. "The only reason that we haven't already been interrupted in these first few minutes is that I told everyone in the office that I wasn't to be disturbed."

"That and the sticky note I saw on your door that said, 'Do Not Disturb!'" Phil laughed.

Helen shrugged. "I do whatever I can." She looked up to the ceiling as if searching for an answer. "If it wasn't for that, I would say I'm interrupted a few times every hour."

Phil scribbled another note. "You mentioned your phone before. Besides e-mail, how many calls do you get in a day?"

"Which phone are you talking about? My office phone or my cell phone?"

"Both."

"Well, I don't give out my cell phone number, except to a few people and family members. My office calls do get screened by the receptionist, so I'd say I don't get too many calls. Maybe one per hour."

"Okay," Phil said. "Just a moment." He began drawing a small picture into his notebook.

Phil turned the notebook around and showed Helen:

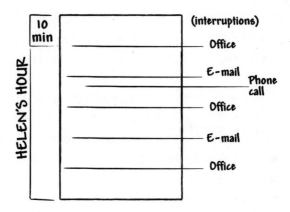

"This is what you've told me your typical work hour looks like. In an average hour, you have about six interruptions. That's one interruption approximately every ten minutes. Is that right?"

Helen stared at the picture, dumbfounded. "Okay. I get what you're saying."

"I actually didn't say anything yet," Phil replied. "All we've done is consider a few questions to discover the truth. So what is the *truth* saying to you?"

11

The average number of minutes an employee can devote to a project before being interrupted.

—Study conducted by the Irvine Department of Information and Computer Science, University of California, Irvine

---

Helen leaned forward, propped her head on her hand, and began pulling her hair through her fingers. "The truth is telling me that my hour is split up way too much. How can anyone get anything done with all that going on? Yet that's what my day is like." Suddenly getting a new thought, she sat up straight and pointed at Phil. "But that's why I multitask!"

Phil sat expressionless. "Go on."

Clearly excited for the chance to defend herself, Helen continued, "With so many different things going on, I have to be prepared to handle them all at once. As a result, I've mastered the art of being able to do more than one thing at once."

"Ah," Phil smiled. "Multitasking is an art now?"

"It is!" Helen exclaimed good-naturedly. "How else can someone get everything done that they need to? Everything happens so fast now: e-mail, voice mail, faxes, Internet, instant messaging, you name it! You've got to move fast to keep up with the roller-coaster."

"Can you give me an example of a typical time you had to multitask?" Phil asked.

Helen thought for a moment. "Sure. Usually I'll be answering e-mail, and someone will come in and ask me a quick question." She smiled. "It's always a quick question."

"So, what do you do?"

"Well, I'll keep working on the e-mail and tell them to go ahead and ask the question. I'll respond to the question, and then I'll go back to work." She looked at Phil, waiting for a reaction. "That's it."

Phil nodded. "So you really didn't multitask, did you?"

"What do you mean?"

"I mean you really weren't doing two things at once. You were *switchtasking*. You switched back and forth between two tasks. It happened so fast that you didn't recognize it, but you were really jumping

> Our . . . research offers neurological evidence that the brain cannot effectively do two things at once.
>
> —René Marois, Ph.D., Department of Psychology, Vanderbilt University, in an interview with the *Vanderbilt Register*

mental tracks during that whole exchange. May I take a guess what was really going on in your mind?

"You were working on the computer. You were probably very focused and getting something accomplished. Then along comes the coworker. You were interrupted. *Switch*.

"You tried to keep typing the e-mail for a moment. Your coworker kept speaking to you, even though you weren't listening. *Switch*.

"You finally gave up and listened to the question. You were doing your best to pay attention, but in the back of your mind, you wanted to be done with it and get back to real work. *Switch*.

"You asked her to repeat the question, once you were *finally* ready to pay full attention. *Switch*.

"After listening to the question, you gave a hurried answer, and then you finally turned your attention back to the computer. *Switch*.

"Because of the break in concentration, you had to find where you were in typing the e-mail. You tried to pick up the train of thought you had before. It took a moment to figure out, but finally you got back to work."

Multitasking: A polite way of telling someone you haven't heard a word they said.

—UrbanDictionary.com, definition submitted by "workinglate."

Helen looked puzzled. "I don't get it. What is your point?"

"My point is that switchtasking is very costly. It is a less effective and less efficient way to get things done." Phil sat back in his chair. "Have you ever studied economics, Helen?"

"Ugh," she grunted. "Let's just say that it wasn't my favorite subject in college."

Phil smiled. "I can appreciate that. Most people hate studying economics. For me, it was a bit of a hobby. I actually read economics books for fun."

"Wow, you really are weird," Helen joked.

"I know. I know." Phil shrugged in self-deprecation. "In economics, they teach a principle called *switching cost*. The switching cost usually refers to the cost of switching from one supplier to another. Let's imagine you switched from that supplier in Kansas that Sally mentioned to one in China. What would be the costs to your company?"

"Wow," Helen replied. "They would be huge. It would cost us a lot of time learning all about the new supplier. We might even have to learn a new language. We might save on the products, but it might cost us more on shipping. We would have to learn a lot of new things. We're not ready for that at all."

Switching costs result when people must go back and review what they've done before they can resume work on a task. The more complicated the task . . . the greater the cost.

—Time Management, Harvard Business School

"Of course," Phil said. "The switching costs could make it a poor decision for your company to make that kind of switch, at least at this moment.

"The same rules apply when you switchtask. Any time you switch from one activity or thought process to another, there is a cost. This cost isn't nearly as large as, say, switching from Kansas to China. Yet there is still a cost. We could call it a *micro-switching cost*."

Helen nodded. "I think I follow you."

"Great. So let's go back and analyze your example of the interrupted e-mail. What were the switching costs?"

"Well," Helen said thoughtfully, "I believe it cost me just a little time when I broke concentration on the e-mail to stop and listen to my employee. But because I wasn't really paying attention to the question, I lost time. I had to ask the employee to repeat the question. Then when she repeated it and I finally paid attention, I had to switch again." She sat pondering for a moment. "I had completely lost the thought process I had before, so then I had to find my place in the e-mail. Finally, I began typing again. Wow."

> We found that the longer a worker is distracted by an interruption, the more likely that they will continue to be interrupted and not resume the task in that same day.
>
> —Study conducted by the Irvine Department of Information and Computer Science, University of California, Irvine

Phil could begin to see the recognition on Helen's face. "How much did time that *quick* question really cost you, Helen?"

Helen gasped, "Probably about five minutes!"

"Exactly."

Phil picked up the drawing of "Helen's Hour" again. "Let's take a look at this picture again, Helen. Each one of these vertical lines in the hour represents a switch. Before we take a look at how much time you lost, let's talk about the different kinds of switches you made.

"Some of these switches you initiated. We'll call these *active switches*. These are times you decided to switch tasks to make a call, get up from your desk to go talk to someone, or decided to check e-mail on your own. Anytime you are the one making the switch, it is an active switch.

"The rest of the switches are *passive switches*. These were initiated by someone or something other than you. Examples of passive interruptions are automatic e-mail arrival notifications, the cell phone ringing, or someone walking into your office without an appointment."

Most common interruptions at work:

1. A colleague stopping by
2. Being called away or leaving desk voluntarily
3. The arrival of new e-mail
4. Switching to another task on the computer
5. A phone call

—Study conducted by the Irvine Department of Information and Computer Science, University of California, Irvine

Helen sighed and shook her head. "For me, I bet the passive interruptions are the worst."

"Possibly," Phil added. "Generally the more extensive a person's job description, the more responsibility for management a person has, the more they are assaulted by passive interruptions. So in your case, it wouldn't surprise me."

Helen pointed toward the door. "But how do I keep people from bugging me all day long. I can't! Without my input, everything starts to fall apart."

Phil held his hands up indicating that Helen needed to slow down. "We'll get to the solutions to your problem in a bit. First, let's take a look at the consequence of all these passive and active switches. Imagine that in the hour we're discussing, you're reviewing the financials of the company." Phil pointed to the first line with the word *office* next to it. "The first switchtask occurred when someone came into your office at ten minutes into the hour and interrupted your review. When we discussed the interrupted e-mail example, you estimated that, on average, you lose five minutes." Phil wrote *5 minutes* on the diagram.

He continued, "After you got back to reviewing your financials, the next switchtask occurred when your e-mail program beeped at you and told you that new messages had arrived." He pointed to the *e-mail* line. "What would you guess is the average switching cost for checking your e-mail?"

Helen tapped the table with her pen in thought. "I would guess that's not too bad. Most of the time I just look and get back to it later." She trailed off and then put on a guilty smile. "Unless it's something important. Then I answer the e-mail right then. I guess on average it's probably another five minutes."

Phil wrote *5 minutes* next to the *e-mail* line.

"Then a phone call comes in, causing you to switchtask again," Phil said, pointing to the phone call line. "Notice that now we're starting to overlap? We've got three tasks going simultaneously: reviewing the financials, answering an e-mail, and someone has just called you. What is the average switching cost for an incoming call?"

"Well, if it's my cell phone, it's family. Then it's probably an emergency, usually one of my sons getting in trouble at school again," Helen mumbled. "If it's on my office phone, my receptionist just asks if I want to take the call. I can, of course, tell her to have them call back later."

"Delaying the inevitable," Phil interjected.

"Yes, the inevitable," Helen agreed reluctantly. "Most of the time I end up taking phone calls unrelated to the task I'm working on. I have to take them because they're important. I would guess phone calls average about seven minutes."

"Okay. I'm just going to assign five minutes of switching cost to each of the other switches. Is that okay?"

"Sure," Helen nodded.

"That brings us to a total switching cost of thirty-two minutes." Phil jotted a few more notes down. "Let's look at what we have."

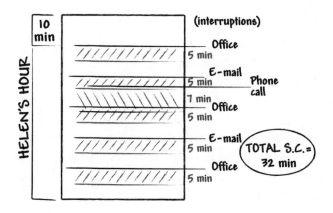

Phil paused for a moment to let Helen soak it in. Then, finally, he said, "Tell me what you see, Helen."

Helen shook her head in disgust. "I see a mess! How can anyone get anything done in that hour?"

"Go on," Phil said quietly.

"If I add up all the blank spaces in that hour, I'm only able to focus on the financials for a total of about thirty minutes!" Helen was shifting in her chair. "And on top of that, the longest period of time I'm ever able to be uninterrupted, or not switchtasking, is ten minutes at the beginning of the hour. After that, I can only work for five minutes at a time!"

Phil nodded. "You're beginning to see the picture. The research backs you up, Helen. Studies have shown that on average, each person loses about 28 percent of the workday due to interruptions and inefficiencies. Multitasking—or switchtasking—is probably the biggest culprit.

> *I, more than anybody I've ever met, do not believe in multitasking. I think it's the absolute ruination of the perfection of a project.*
>
> —Suze Orman, author and financial planner

"Consider what you are paying your employees, Helen. Consider your payroll expense. If your employees are similar in their work patterns to the studies, 28 percent of that payroll is just being thrown away."

"What about *me?* This drawing is telling me that I'm losing about 50 percent of my time!" Helen exclaimed.

"True," Phil agreed,

2.1 hours

Average estimated lost productivity per person per day due to interruptions, based on a 40-hour workweek

$650 billion

Estimated annual loss to the U.S. economy due to unnecessary interruptions plus recovery time

—Interview with Jonathan B. Spira, CEO and chief analyst of Basex Research

"and that is because you are the CEO. Remember this rule: the more responsibility you have, the more hats you wear, the more likely you are to become inefficient. It's a law of switchtasking.

THE ORIGIN

Helen stretched and rubbed her arms as if she had just been through a workout. Then she shook her head at Phil. "I don't get it. If multitasking is such a bad thing, then why does everyone do it?"

"Basically it's because the word itself is incorrect. Around the end of the twentieth century, some wordsmith saw the connection between our increasingly hectic world and the world of a computer. A catchword was born. Newspapers began peppering their articles with the word. Talk show hosts began using it with frequency. Magazines began publishing articles about how to multitask more effectively. Multitasking quickly became as popular and accepted as the automobile and the hamburger.

"Yet the word *multitasking* was originally never used for the way humans operate. Let's look it up on the Internet." Phil gestured to Helen's computer.

"Where should I search?" Helen asked as she moved back to her corner desk.

"Go to the Wikipedia site and search for *multitasking*."

Helen pulled up her Web browser and went to wikipedia.org. She typed in the word *multitasking* and then hit Enter. "Here's the first definition: 'the apparent simultaneous performance of two or more tasks by a computer's central processing unit.' Sounds like something my IT guy would say." Helen chuckled.

"Exactly," Phil agreed. "Multitasking was first a computing term. The word *apparent* in that definition is very important. Just like your brain, the computer really can't focus on two or more things at the same time. What the processor is really doing is switching rapidly between one program and the other, giving

In multitasking, only one CPU is involved, but it switches from one program to another so quickly that it gives the appearance of executing all of the programs at the same time.

—Internet.com Webopedia

the illusion that it's doing it all at the same time." Phil thought for a moment. "Of course, your IT guy could explain it all in much greater depth."

Helen rolled her eyes. "Oh, I know. More than I need to hear. Your explanation is good enough. Go on."

"As you can see, we humans really need to use better words to describe what we're doing," Phil continued. "I've already talked to you about switchtasking. That's when you're trying to perform two or more tasks at the same time that require mental effort."

"Like answering e-mail and trying to listen to a coworker. Or talking on the phone and reviewing the financials," Helen added.

"You've got it," Phil nodded. "Yet there is another term that describes a productive use of time doing multiple things. It's called *background tasking.*"

"Background tasking?" Helen asked. "What's that?"

Phil continued, "Background tasking is when you perform two or more tasks where only one of those tasks requires mental effort. Examples of background tasking could be eating dinner and watching TV, or jogging and listening to music."

"What about working on something on your computer while your printer is working on a large print job?" Helen asked.

"That is a perfect example of background tasking," Phil replied.

"What about talking on the phone while driving?"

Phil laughed. "I've been doing this long enough to be careful around that subject. It's a touchy area for a lot of people. I've heard of studies that reported talking and driving is as bad as drinking and driving, but it's not clear yet."

"All I know is that usually when someone is driving like a maniac on the road and I pass them, they're holding a phone in their hands!" Helen exclaimed.

"Well, there you go," Phil said. "From your perspective, driving and talking on the phone is switchtasking, not background tasking."

"So is background tasking good and switchtasking bad?" Helen asked.

Phil held up a cautionary finger as he responded. "I would never use the words *good* or *bad*. Switchtasking is always less efficient and less effective. Background tasking, on the other hand, has the potential to be efficient and effective." Phil quickly added, "If it is used properly."

"But when most people talk about multitasking, they're not talking about background tasking, are they, Phil?"

Phil shook his head. "You're right. When most people refer to multitasking, they are really talking about switchtasking. No matter how they do it, switching rapidly between two things is just not very efficient or effective."

THE EXERCISE

Suddenly there was a knock at the door. Helen grimaced and gestured to the door. "You see, Phil?"

Without waiting for a response, the door opened a crack, then gradually some more. Sally, the woman wearing glasses, poked her head in. "I'm really sorry, Helen. I know you said you didn't want to be disturbed. I just have a very quick question."

Helen still had her focus on Phil. "Okay, Mr. Multitasking Expert. What am I supposed to do?"

"It's your decision how you use my time, Helen," Phil replied. "I'm at your disposal. However, my time is limited. One question you could ask yourself is, 'What will be the switching cost of this interruption?'"

Helen nodded reluctantly and then turned to Sally. "Can this wait, Sally? I mean, is it an emergency?"

Sally sighed. It was obvious to Phil that she had become accustomed to constantly being put off by Helen. "It's just a quick question. You can go right back to what you're doing. What's the big deal?"

"The big deal," Helen jumped in, "is that multitasking is a lie. You're asking me to switch attention, and that makes me less productive."

Sally grunted in disgust. "Did *he* tell you that?" She pointed an accusing finger at Phil, who raised his eyebrows in surprise.

Helen rolled her eyes. "Yes, Sally. Phil just explained how multitasking is hurting me more than helping me."

Sally snorted. "Of course, he did. He's a *man*. Men can't multitask, but for women, it's a way of life. It's proven that women are better multitaskers than men."

Phil smiled and tried his best to appear genuinely surprised. "Really? Wow. I wasn't aware of that. Where did you hear that?"

Sally paused and closed one eye, searching her mind for the right answer. "A friend told me about it once. I can't remember where she said she heard it. Maybe it was a magazine article. A TV show?"

Phil nodded. "To be honest, this isn't the first time I've heard about the men versus women multitasking debate." He was speaking now to both Helen and Sally. Phil spoke with a bit more caution, finding himself outnumbered. "There are certainly many studies that show that the brain chemistry among individuals, including men and women, can vary greatly. Some studies have shown that male rats seem to be more 'single-minded' than female rats."

"There you go!" Sally jumped in.

"However," Phil continued steadily, "those same studies show no advantage when it comes to multitasking. When those same studies were replicated with humans, the results were hazy. There is a lack of evidence demonstrating a gender difference when it comes to multitasking."

Helen turned her attention back to Sally, as if observing a tennis match.

Sally was growing agitated. "All I know is that I can handle doing a lot more things at the same time than most men can. Men get frustrated with multitasking. I've been dealing with it my whole life!" She pointed to Helen. "You can't say you haven't seen that, Helen. Don't men seem to have a harder time with multitasking?"

Helen nodded slightly. "I suppose that is true."

Phil sighed and mentally strapped himself into his chair. He saw a bumpy road ahead. After taking a deep breath, he turned to Helen. "Do you have a few pieces of paper we can use? I'd like to show you something that will help us with our little debate." Helen grabbed some paper from the printer tray and handed a sheet to Sally. Phil continued, "Sally, do you have a moment to do a brief exercise with us?"

> *There was no evidence whatsoever of any gender difference in performance.*
>
> —David E. Meyer, Ph.D., Department of Psychology, University of Michigan, in an interview with CNN

"How long is this going to take? I have a lot to do."

"I don't doubt you do," Phil replied. "This will only take about three minutes."

Wordlessly, Sally plopped into the chair and took the piece of paper that Helen offered. "Okay. Let's see your little example."

Phil turned his paper sideways and drew several lines across it.

"Make your paper look like this," he said.

	Multitasking is worse than a lie
M	
1	
M	
1	

Helen and Sally took a few moments to make their papers look like Phil's. They both wrote the same phrase he had on the top of his paper: *Multitasking is worse than a lie.*

"Okay," Phil began, "what we are going to do is find out which of you is the better multitasker. This exercise is simple. We're going to see how long it takes you to write the phrase *Multitasking is worse than a lie.*

"However, for every letter you copy, you're going to immediately write a number just below it on the next line bottom. For example, you're going to start by writing an *M* in the first row, then a *1* in the second row. Next you write *U* in the first row and *2* in the second row, and so on. Does that make sense?"

"Yes," Helen said. "We write one number, in ascending order, for every letter in the sentence *Multitasking is worse than a lie.*"

"Yes. Just make sure you switch to writing a number after every letter in the sentence." Phil lifted up his wristwatch. "I'm going to time you to see how long it takes for you to complete the exercise."

"What do we do with the bottom two rows on the paper?" Sally asked.

"Just ignore those bottom two rows for now. We'll get to them in a second." Phil held his wristwatch close to his face. "Ready?"

Sally and Helen picked up their pens and leaned over their papers. "Yes," they replied in unison.

"Go!"

Sally and Helen both began writing furiously.

Multitasking: A nice way to say that you're doing many different things at the same time. And since no one can divide by 0, that means you're doing many different things half-a—d.

—UrbanDictionary.com, definition submitted by "Joe Sabs"

The room was silent except for the sound of pens scratching against paper.

A few seconds into their copying, Helen began to giggle. "This is harder than it looks!"

"Aargh!" Sally cried. "I keep messing up."

Phil looked carefully at their papers, watching their progress. As Helen finished writing her last number, a 27, Phil shot out quickly, "Sixty seconds." Sally finished just a moment later, and Phil said, "Sixty-three seconds. Okay, both of you write your times down on your paper at the end of the second row."

	Multitasking is worse than a lie
M	Multi*t*asking is worse than a lie
1	1 2 3 4 5 6 7 8 9 10 11 12 13 14 15 16 17 18 19 20 21 22 23 24 25 26 27 _(63 sec)_
M	
1	

"I feel like I'm taking a test at school again," Helen laughed. Sally nodded in reluctant agreement.

"All right. Ready for the next step?" Phil asked. "Now we're going to write the same thing in the bottom two rows. You're going to copy the phrase *Multitasking is worse than a lie*, and then write the number sequence from 1 to 27. This time, however, you're not going to switch between each letter. Just write each row from start to finish. Got it?"

Helen and Sally were already poised to go again. They both gave quick nods to show they were ready.

"Go!"

This time Sally and Helen wrote as quickly as before, yet they both seemed more relaxed.

"Twenty-nine seconds," Phil said as the women finished in unison. "Both of you finished at the same time. Write down *29 seconds* at the end of the fourth row."

Sally had grown quiet. She was staring at her paper with a hint of disbelief on her face.

After a moment, she said quietly, "I could tell where you were going with this. I could see the first time was taking longer, but I didn't realize it would take me twice as long!"

Phil turned his head casually to Helen. "Do you want to take a stab at explaining this to her?"

	Multitasking is worse than a lie
M	*Multi*_t*asking is worse than a lie*
1	1 2 3 4 5 6 7 8 9 10 11 12 13 14 15 16 17 18 19 20 22 23 25 27 (63 sec) 19 21 24 26
M	*Multitasking is worse than a lie*
1	1 2 3 4 5 6 7 8 9 10 11 12 13 14 15 16 17 18 19 20 21 22 23 24 25 (29 sec) 26 27

Helen cleared her throat. "Well, it's a switching cost, right?" Phil nodded. "What we just did is pretty much the same as multitasking. We were attempting to do two things at the same time. Every time we switched back and forth between the letters and the numbers, there was a cost. The movement of the pens was costing us a little here and a little there."

"Don't forget the mental switch," Phil said casually.

> The brain is a lot like a computer. You may have several screens open on your desktop, but you're able to think about only one at a time.
>
> —William R. Stixrud, Ph.D., neuropsychologist, in an interview with Scholastic.com

"Every time you went back and forth, you had to remember where you were."

"Right," Helen nodded. "I think for me that was the biggest cost, not to mention that I had to repeat some work because of all the mistakes I made."

Sally was examining her own mistakes on her worksheet. Still staring at the paper, she asked, "Well, not all multitasking is bad, is it? I mean it helps me get a lot done."

Helen and Phil looked at each other and smiled. "I'll explain background tasking to her later," Helen told Phil with a wink.

"This isn't about good and bad, Sally," Phil explained. "This is about what is effective and efficient."

Sally was quiet.

"However," Phil continued quickly, "my experience is that most people multitask—"

"Switchtask!" Helen corrected.

"Thank you," Phil smiled. "People tend to switch-task in situations when it is highly inappropriate."

THE EXAMPLE

Sally had been staring outside the office window for several moments. She said, "I think I see an example of what you're talking about right now. Look outside the window."

Helen and Phil turned to look at what Sally was staring at. Through the window of Helen's second-story office, they could see into the cubicles on the first floor. A young man wearing a college sweatshirt was standing in a coworker's cubicle. From his posture, Phil could tell he was trying to convey a very important point to his female coworker.

"Look at Tracy," Sally said. Tracy, the coworker on the floor, was poring over what looked like a company report while she gave half an ear to the young man. "Is she even listening to Jason?"

"Jason is an intern here," Helen explained to Phil. "He does good work for us, but he's a little overeager sometimes. Tracy is his supervisor at the moment."

Jason continued to speak with enthusiasm as Tracy interjected a word or two without looking up from her documents. Abruptly she reached for her belt pouch that held her cell phone and picked it up. She began walking away from Jason as she took the call.

Jason stood dejectedly as he watched Tracy walk off. He shook his head and then shuffled back to his cubicle.

> *No matter how busy you are, you must take time to make the other person feel important.*
>
> —Mary Kay Ash

"Poor guy," Sally said sympathetically. Helen looked at Sally out of the corner of her eye. Phil couldn't tell for sure, but he got the impression that Helen doubted her sincerity.

As the scene downstairs concluded, Phil spoke softly. "It's bad enough losing efficiency and effectiveness when we try to multitask. But often we multitask—switchtask—when another human being is involved. And that always has a very high cost.

"The people we live with and work with on a daily basis deserve our full attention. When we give people segmented attention, piecemeal time, switching back and forth, the switching cost is higher than just the time involved. We end up damaging relationships."

He paused and looked at the women carefully. They were both suddenly very somber.

Sally was the first to break the silence. "I have to admit it. That's an area where I need to improve. I don't give people the attention they want."

> *[We] will never, ever be able to overcome the inherent limitations in the brain for processing information during multitasking. It just can't be, any more than the best of all humans will ever be able to run a one-minute mile.*
>
> —David E. Meyer, Ph.D., Department of Psychology, University of Michigan, in an interview with *Time*

Phil smiled encouragingly. "We all have done it, Sally. We'll all continue to do it as long as we accept multitasking—switchtasking—as acceptable.

"The point is this: when someone tells me that they are good at multitasking, I know they're inefficient. Saying that you're a good multitasker is the same as saying that you're good at using a less effective method to get things done.

"It's like saying, 'Bob is better at riding a bike than Chuck is at driving a car.' Even if that statement is true, Chuck is still going to reach his destination with greater speed and greater ease than Bob.

"No matter how effective you are at switchtasking, you are still working less efficiently than you could another way. You are going to take longer to get things done than the person who focuses on one attention-requiring activity at a time."

THE QUESTION

After the trio turned away from the window, Sally got her chance to ask Helen her question. Phil noticed Helen was now giving Sally increased attention.

Before Sally left, however, she paused again, scrunching her eyebrows as if trying to remember something. As a moment or two passed, nothing apparently occurred to her.

"Sally, before you leave, do you mind if I ask you something?" Phil asked.

"Sure, Phil."

"The last two times I've seen you about to leave this room, you stopped and paused for a while," he said. "You looked as if you were trying to remember something. Do you mind if I ask why?"

Sally looked surprised. "Do I do that? I've never noticed." She rubbed her head. "I guess it's because I'm not sure I've asked Helen everything I need to ask. I want to make sure I get it all out while I've got the chance." She shrugged. "Does that answer your question?"

"Perfectly." Phil smiled.

"Thank you, Sally," Helen said.

Phil watched Sally thoughtfully as she closed the door behind her. He turned back toward Helen. "Is that pretty typical behavior for anyone who comes into your office? Do they pause after talking with you and take their time to make sure they've covered everything?"

"I suppose so." Helen paused to think to herself for a moment. "Yes. Now that I think about it, you're right. That is what almost everyone does. My employees seem to try to squeeze every little bit out of me before they leave. Sometimes I pretty much need to shove them out the door before I can get back to work!"

Phil nodded again, smiling to himself. "The reason that they do that can be summed up in one word." Phil reached over and grabbed his notebook. He then wrote a single word on the paper:

WHEN

"*When?*" Helen looked puzzled. "What do you mean?"

"They don't know when they are going to get a chance to talk to you again. Your employees have become used to you being in perpetual switchtasking mode." Phil added a large question mark to the paper:

WHEN?

Phil continued, "Because they don't know when you are ever going to slow down enough to listen to them again, they are afraid. Your employees have learned that once they've grabbed your attention, they shouldn't let go."

Helen scrunched up her chin in concern. "What can I do? I can't always be available for them. That's why I have to close my door. Otherwise people will always come in and ask me questions." Helen sighed in frustration.

Phil erased the question mark on the notepad and then drew a line. It now read:

"If you give your employees a clear *when*, a *when* they can count on, then the fear goes away. They will learn to count on that *when*, and they will learn to hold off most of the questions they have. If your employees learn to rely on the *when* rather than on urgency to talk to you, you will see a large drop in switchtasking."

"How do I give my employees a *when?*" Helen was growing a bit frustrated. "Most of the time I'm so out of control myself that I can't control what happens in my day."

Phil began to speak in slower, softer tones, trying to compensate for Helen's distress. "There are two simple ways to create clear *whens* for your employees." Phil wrote two bullet points on the piece of paper below the large *when*:

WHEN

- Set recurring meetings
- Give a clear expectation of availability

Helen looked the bullet points over carefully. She read them twice. "Okay. What does this mean?"

THE MEETING

"First, let's talk about recurring meetings," Phil explained. "Let's use Sally as our example. I'm guessing Sally is someone you need to meet with frequently."

A smile played across Helen's mouth. "If ten times every day counts as 'frequently,' then I would agree."

"Got it." Phil gave Helen a quick thumbs-up. "Since you meet with Sally several times per day, then I'm going to guess you would need a daily recurring meeting with her for thirty minutes."

"Are you sure that's enough?" Helen asked. "We spend a lot more time than that talking every day."

Phil continued calmly, anticipating Helen's question. "Keep in mind that because you've been switchtasking, the time you've been spending with Sally has been extremely inefficient until this point. You're probably spending twice as much time talking than what you really need."

"Or longer," Helen snorted.

Phil smiled in agreement. "I'm using thirty minutes daily as a guesstimate. You are free to change this at any time, depending on your need.

"Back to the meeting. If you were to set up a thirty-minute meeting with Sally daily, what would be the best possible time to do it? When would be a time that would work for both your schedules?"

Helen tapped the table with a finger. "Well, I'm guessing it would probably be one hour after Sally gets in. That's usually when she starts finding all sorts of fires for me to put out, so let's say 10:00 A.M."

"Great." Phil wrote *once daily, 30 minutes, 10:00 A.M.* on the paper under the *recurring meeting* bullet point. "You've just created a *when* for Sally. Once you set this daily meeting up with her, she'll then know when to expect she'll get a chance to talk with you."

"Oh, I see," Helen remarked.

"This simple recurring meeting is like magic, Helen." Phil began to speak with more enthusiasm.

"When my clients have set this meeting up with their employees, the switching slows down considerably. The sporadic interruptions start to disappear as if by magic. Why do you think this happens?"

Phil waited patiently while Helen considered her response. "My guess," she replied, "is that it's because Sally would now know that she will have a chance to talk with me. She'll hold off on most of her questions until that meeting. Is that right?"

"You've got it," Phil said approvingly. "Of course, if there is an actual emergency, then she'll let you know before then. However, the majority of what happens in business isn't really an emergency. Normal occurrences have grown to feel like emergencies to your employees because they fear that they'll never be able to talk to you about them.

"The trick is that you have to be prepared for those meetings and have a system in place to know what you'll be discussing ahead of time. However, that's a conversation for another day."

"Do I need to set up a recurring meeting with *everyone* in my company?" Helen laughed. "All I'll be doing is having meetings!"

Phil smiled. "You need recurring meetings only with those people who are accountable to you or have regular questions for you." Phil wrote the phrases *accountable* and *regular questions* under the *once daily* bullet point.

"How often should we meet?" Helen asked.

"Someone who is interrupting you once a day right now may need one meeting a week. Maybe less," Phil answered.

"So the more attention the employee needs, the more often we should meet," Helen confirmed.

"Exactly," Phil said. "However, most of my clients have found that an hour-long meeting, twice per month, is perfect for employees who report directly to them."

THE EXPECTATION

Helen looked at Phil with growing intrigue. "Okay, so tell me about the second point. You wrote *give a clear expectation of availability.*"

"Right," Phil continued. "This second point applies to the interruptions that aren't emergencies but come from people with whom you don't have a recurring meeting: unexpected phone calls, incidental questions, drop-in visits, and so on."

Helen grumbled, "That is about half my day. How do I give an expectation when so much of my day seems random?"

"Maybe you've seen those signs hanging on the doors of some businesses that say, 'We'll be back at . . .' and then give a time?" Phil asked.

"You mean the signs with little clock hands that adjust?" Helen asked.

Phil nodded.

"Sure," she said. "They have one at my hair salon."

"Great. What is the purpose of that clock?" Phil asked. "It sets an expectation, right? Even most large retail chains have a sign that displays store hours. Essentially what I'm suggesting, Helen, is that you post your personal store hours. When are you *personally* open for business?"

"What do you mean?" Helen asked. "If people know when I'm going to be available, they'll just wait to talk to me then?"

"Pretty much," Phil replied. "It's not your unavailability that makes people nervous and causes them to interrupt you. It's the uncertainty of when they'll get a chance to talk to you that makes them worry. Because your employees don't have any idea when you are open for business, so to speak, they are beating down your door at all hours of the day.

"The most difficult part about this will be the first time you change people's expectations."

"I see," Helen said to herself. "Since I've been letting people get away with interrupting me for a long time, they're going to resist the change. I've been doing it all wrong."

"Not 'wrong,' Helen," Phil corrected. "Just not very efficiently." He reached down to the floor and picked up his briefcase. He opened it, searched for a moment, and then pulled out a thin plastic sign with clock hands. "I just happen to have one of those shop signs for you, Helen. Consider it a gift. Just hang this on your door when you don't want to be disturbed. Be sure to indicate the time when you'll be available."

> *Multitasking? I can't even do two things at once. I can't even do one thing at once.*
>
> —Helena Bonham Carter

Helen laughed. "This is great! Thank you!"

"You're welcome."

After a pause, Helen continued, "So what about phone calls? If you remember, that was a big cause for me to switchtask."

Phil looked at his watch, then picked up his mobile phone, and began dialing a number. "I'm calling a client of mine right now." Phil switched his cell phone to speakerphone.

"Listen."

After the fourth ring, a pleasant, professional male voice began speaking:

"Hello, this is James. You've reached my voice mail, which means I'm probably meeting with a customer right now. I do check my messages frequently, usually at 10:00 A.M., 2:00 P.M., and 4:00 P.M. If you leave a message, I will be sure to get back to you before the day is over. Thank you!"

Phil hung up the phone.

Helen exclaimed, "Wow! Does he really do that? Return calls at those times? And his customers are okay with that?"

Phil clasped his hands together and nodded with a smile. "He follows that schedule every day like a finely tuned clock. In the beginning, it took his coworkers and customers by surprise, particularly because he used to be a complete mess."

"Not as bad as me," Helen grunted.

"Worse, actually," Phil said bluntly. "He was in constant firefighting mode, jumping from call to call, from interruption to interruption. He was a poster child for switchtasking."

Helen sat in stunned silence.

"Yet now those same coworkers and customers have much more respect for him. They have come to rely on him as dependable. He returns every call in a timely manner. He just doesn't try to return them all at the same time, or in the middle of a meeting, or while answering e-mail.

"The key for him—and for you, Helen—is that he uses his calendar to determine *in advance* when he is going to deal with the interruptions to his day."

"He doesn't switchtask," Helen quietly added.

Phil nodded. "There is an illusion that so many people buy into," Phil continued. "The illusion is that technology, cell phones, e-mail, faxes, text messaging, and whatever is latest-and-greatest all make us more productive.

"The reality, though, is that these things will make us productive only if we learn to take control of them. They are the servants. We are the masters. If you and I don't set up a schedule and protect our time, we allow ourselves to be run over by the traffic of information."

THE TRUTH

Phil pulled out a small USB drive and handed it to Helen. "Before we wrap up our training for today, there is one more exercise I would like to take you through. Can you print out this file?"

"Okay," Helen agreed as she walked over to the computer. "Anything to get me out of the habit of switchtasking." Her printer hummed as it began its job.

"I've found people change their behavior when they understand the simple truth about where they are. Once you see the truth about how you are using time, you'll have more clarity about you want to do instead."

Phil grabbed the paper from the printer and showed it to Helen:

ACTIVITY	BOUNDARY
Lost Time	Scratching nose, getting up from a chair, and so on
Sleep	Total hours of actual sleep, including daytime naps
Prep	Showering, dressing, and so on, morning and night
Work	Primary job work-related activities, including travel to and from office
Personal Recreation	

CURRENT	FUTURE
7	7

"What we are going to do is fairly simple," Phil explained, "and it should tell us a lot about how you are spending your time."

"At work?" Helen asked.

"In your life as a whole," Phil replied. "We can talk about each activity that you perform at work in a future meeting. You'll notice that the worksheet already has a few categories that all people have in common."

"I'm ready to go." Helen stretched her fingers in front of the paper.

Phil grinned. "First, we'll fill out the Activity column. In this column, we're going to broadly list all the different things you do in an average week."

"What does *Lost Time* mean?" Helen pointed to the first activity listed.

"Lost time is the average time that everyone loses in a day doing things we barely notice," Phil explained. "As the chart describes in the Boundary column, this includes things such as scratching your nose, getting up from a chair, adjusting your clothes, going to the bathroom, and so on. Each person loses about an hour per day."

"Okay, so I'm supposed to categorize all of the activities that I do on a weekly basis." Helen stared blankly at the paper for a few moments. "Can you help me out here? What are some categories that other people list?"

"Some that I've seen include family time, community or church service, housework, dates with spouse, or even specific time-consuming hobbies such as playing in band or basketball team," Phil offered.

"Got it," Helen said abruptly as she began writing in her column. After a few minutes, Helen said, "Done."

"Great," Phil said. "Now, let's move to the Boundary column. You notice that several of these are already filled out. For instance, next to Work, it says, *Primary job work-related activities, including travel to and from office.*"

"You included travel in the work category?" Helen sounded surprised.

"Right. It's a preference. Some people would, some wouldn't. For clarity, I included travel time as part of the Work category. The idea is that we don't want to have any category overlapping or any time counted twice.

"For instance," Phil continued, "some people would say that family time includes dates with their spouse, while others might say that family time is time with their children, and that going on a date with the spouse deserves its own category.

"It really doesn't matter how you want to define the boundaries between the activities. The only thing that matters is that you are clear about the differences between each category. This will help a lot when we begin estimating your time use."

"Okay," Helen said. "So for me, personal recreation means the time I spend just doing my own thing. For instance, I like to scrapbook occasionally, so I wrote that in Boundary. Is that right?"

Phil nodded to Helen. She continued to write a few lines in the Boundary column for each category.

When she finished, Phil looked over her worksheet briefly and said, "Great job. The next thing we need to do is estimate how much time—per week—you're currently spending in each activity. You'll notice that Lost Time is already filled out for you in the Current and Futures columns, at an average of one hour per day for a total of seven hours per week.

"The next category listed is Sleep. Since this is one of the easiest to figure, let's start here. How much sleep do you get in an average day?"

Helen laughed. "Not as much as I need, that's for sure!" She thought for a moment and then wrote the number *49* in the Current column for sleep. "I figure about six hours on weeknights, then a little more on the weekends, for an average of seven hours per night."

"Sounds reasonable to me." Phil pointed to the next row. "Go ahead and fill out how much time you're spending in each of the other activities. Make sure to keep an eye on the Boundary column and not double-count any of your time.

"One last piece of instruction: don't worry about the total right now. Just give it your best guess. We'll adjust the total at the end."

Helen spent the next ten minutes scribbling notes onto the worksheet. She erased her first guess several times and adjusted her estimates. Finally, she sat back and said, "All right, I'm done."

Phil didn't even glance at her paper as he asked, "Now before we go any further, I want you to take a look at your estimates for each activity. Do your estimates look reasonable to you?"

Helen carefully looked over the chart and said, "Sure. It looks right to me. What's the total?"

Phil pulled out a small calculator and added everything up. "The total is 190, Helen." He paused. "Do you know how many hours there are in a week?"

Helen thought for a moment, again using her fingers slightly to do the math. "Is it 168 hours in a week? Boy, was I off!"

Phil leaned back in his chair and took a deep breath. "Part of the reason we do this exercise is to gauge how well you can estimate time. People who engage in switchtasking over a long period of time begin to get a distorted sense of how long things actually take."

Helen threw her hands up in the air. "I'm about twenty-two hours per week distorted! No wonder I always feel like I'm about a day behind."

Phil slowly pulled the worksheet over to him and wrote the following phrase at the top:

THERE IS ONLY <u>ONE</u> TIME LINE.
THERE IS ONLY <u>ONE</u> YOU.

He pushed the paper back to Helen, who read carefully:

"It's amazing to me how many people try to ignore this basic truth, Helen," Phil said good-naturedly. "You're not alone. Switchtasking is just one of the ways in which people try to violate this truth. Other ways include not scheduling travel time, double-booking, and trying to get 65 minutes worth of work into 60 minutes."

"Or 190 hours worth of work into a 168-hour week!" Helen laughed.

"That is the truth of time, Helen. There are only 60 minutes in one hour, there are only 24 hours in a day, and there are only 168 hours in a week. And no matter how hard you try, no matter what you do, you will never be able to change that. All you can do is find the best way to operate within the time you've been given." Noticing that Helen's mood had suddenly turned somber, Phil added, "Coming to the realization of this simple truth has changed a lot of my clients."

Helen sat quietly for a moment. "So if there are really only 168 hours in a week, then where am I getting this 190 hours figure from? Obviously I'm kidding myself. There are 22 hours per week here that I'm not really doing."

THERE IS ONLY <u>ONE</u> TIME LINE.

ACTIVITY	BOUNDARY
Lost Time	Scratching nose, getting up from a chair, and so on
Sleep	Total hours of actual sleep, including daytime naps
Prep	Showering, dressing, and so on, morning and night
Work	Primary job work-related activities, including travel to and from office
Personal Recreation	Scrapbooking, recreational reading
Family Time	Spending time with kids, husband
Community Service	PTA, fundraisers
Exercise	Treadmill, biking
Church	Attending church, meditation
Home Improvement	Working on yard or house, without family
Friends	Getting together with friends
	TOTAL

THERE IS ONLY <u>ONE</u> YOU.

CURRENT	FUTURE
7	7
49	
7	
70	
8	
28	
5	
4	
4	
5	
3	
190/168	

???

Phil nodded in agreement. "You're exactly right. Let's take a look at your worksheet and figure this out." Phil moved his chair around the table slightly so he could look over Helen's shoulder. "Typically when I see someone who misguesses their time like this, the biggest culprit is going to be found in the biggest areas. Where did you estimate you are spending most of your time?"

Helen pointed to the 70 in the Work row. "You mean this?"

"Possibly." Phil scratched his head. "The second highest activity is sleep, at 49 hours. Do you still think that's accurate?" Helen nodded, and he continued, "You also estimated that you were spending about 28 hours per week in the Family Time activity. That's an average of about 4 hours per day. Is that right?"

"I think so." Helen sounded a bit unsure.

"Can you tell me what spending time with your family is like?" Phil asked.

"Well, I get home around six or seven o'clock. If my kids are home, I eat dinner with them. After dinner, we hang out in the living room and watch TV or something. Of course, I spend more time with them on weekends than I do on weekdays."

A brief sign of recognition flashed across Helen's face. "Except . . ."

"What are you thinking about?"

Helen frowned. "What I'm really doing is reading trade magazines or checking my e-mail." She paused for a least a minute before she continued.

"I'm switchtasking on my family, aren't I?"

Phil sat silently, not daring to move at all. He tried to sound as reassuring as possible as he spoke up: "This exercise is about helping you find the truth about how you use your time. It's not my job to tell you how you should or should not be using your time."

> We set out what's going to be our work time versus our foundation time versus family time, and we'll reassess that . . . sometimes every week.
>
> —Melinda Gates

Helen grew upset, though it was not directed at Phil. "But that isn't how I should be spending my time. I'm telling myself that. The sad thing is that it's been like this for a long time. I thought I was being a good parent by being home with my children, but really I was working the whole time. I've been there with my children, but I really haven't been there *for* them."

> *To do two things at once is to do neither.*
>
> —Publilius Syrus, Roman philosopher

Helen paused for a moment, and then sighed. "Now I know why the way Tracy was dealing with Jason bothered me so much. It's the way I deal with my kids! I practically ignore them. Then they give me the same look Jason gave Tracy." She shook her head. "That's really sad."

Phil asked quietly, "Is spending more focused time with your family a priority to you?"

Helen nodded slowly. "It is. It really is."

"I can see that," Phil affirmed. "The great news is that you now have an opportunity. Now that you understand the truth about time, you can make a choice. Now that you understand how you've been spending time in the past, you can make a new time budget."

Helen nodded absently to herself.

Phil pointed toward the last column on the chart titled Future: "Here is the place for you to put things as you would like them to be. You are the one in control of your calendar. Is it all right if I give you a little homework?"

"Sure," Helen said.

"Tonight, take a few quiet moments to yourself, and create a future time budget for yourself. This will represent how you plan to spend your time starting at the beginning of next month." Phil wrote the number 168 at the bottom of the column. "Just make sure it totals up to 168 hours."

"Why next month?" Helen asked. "Why not tomorrow?"

Phil smiled. "If you can put this new budget into action before next month, then that is outstanding. However, my experience is that this kind of change rarely happens overnight. It will probably take a few weeks to make the transition. I can help you set up some systems that will help you be more efficient."

"I'll be sure to do this assignment tonight," Helen said positively.

"Great," Phil said. "We're at the end of our appointment for today, Helen. However, I'd like to follow up with you about this assignment. Would that be all right with you?"

Helen reached for her calendar. "Yes. I want to meet with you again. Can we meet at the same time? 9:00 A.M.?"

"Great." Phil marked the appointment on his calendar. "I'll see you in the morning."

THE DEAL

Phil opened the door of his car and tossed his briefcase to the passenger side. As he was about to shut the car door, he heard a shout from the entrance of GreenGarb.

"Phil, wait!" Sally jogged out to the parking lot. "I'm glad I caught you. I had to ask you a question." She leaned on the car door as she spoke.

Phil turned his neck awkwardly to look at Sally. "No problem. What can I help you with?"

"Well, I was just having a discussion with Tracy. We think you're wrong."

"Okay," Phil said cautiously.

"Look," Sally continued, "it's fine to have a discussion in a controlled office where Helen and you are alone and discussing things. I've seen it before.

Some consultant trains Helen on a concept or two. She has someone give us a rah-rah speech. We get pumped up for a week, and then everything's back to normal."

"Seminar letdown," Phil said absently.

"Huh?"

"I call that seminar letdown when people get excited and then don't follow through." Phil craned his neck even more to look at Sally squarely. "It sounds like your problem isn't with the concept of switchtasking though."

"Well, I can see that I need to pay attention to people more when I'm talking to them," she admitted. "I also agree that having a little more focus would help me out. All I'm saying is that we've got to deal with the real world here! I've been with this company since the beginning. Helen hasn't changed for years."

"I really do understand where you're coming from, Sally." Phil stared at her for a moment. "How about we make a deal?"

Sally removed her arm from the car door and looked at Phil skeptically. "What kind of food do you like?" Phil asked.

"Food? Well, I know I don't look like it," Sally said, referring to her somewhat thin frame, "but I'm a meat-and-potatoes girl. I like steak."

"And what's the best steakhouse around here?"

"The best? The best is Carvemasters."

Phil pulled out his notepad and jotted a few notes. "Here's the deal. I'll follow up with you in a couple of months, and you report to me how Helen is doing. You tell me what kind of progress Helen has made. If nothing has changed, I'll buy you a gift certificate for dinner for two at Carvemasters. This will completely be on your honor. I expect honest feedback.

"If, however, Helen has made significant positive change, then you need to bake me a dozen chocolate chip cookies."

Sally chortled. "That's dangerous! You don't know how I cook."

Phil winked, "I doubt a meat-and-potatoes girl doesn't know how to bake cookies." Phil stuck out his hand. "Sound fair?"

"Make mine medium rare!" Sally declared as she shook Phil's hand enthusiastically.

THE CHANGE

When Phil arrived the next morning, the receptionist greeted him warmly. "Yes, Ms. Whitman is expecting you. You know the way, yes?"

Phil wandered down the hallway again and found his way back to Helen's office. This time the door was open, and no one was inside. Phil found his chair at the table and sat down to wait.

He didn't wait long before Helen suddenly burst into the room, her face full of excitement. "I'll have you know that I spent time with my family last night, and I didn't switchtask! I got home and said, 'Let's go out to dinner." My kids were surprised. We went to the restaurant, and I paid attention to them. I didn't think about anything else but spending time with my family. It was wonderful!"

Phil clapped his hands in praise for Helen. "Way to go! What did they think?"

"At first, I don't think they took me seriously. They asked what the special occasion was!" Helen shook her head with a smile. "After they realized that I was really spending time with them and paying attention to them, they were excited. I could tell they really appreciated it."

"I'm sure they did," Phil agreed. "It's not unusual for someone to be surprised when they see a change in your behavior like that. Over time, when they've seen that you're no longer multitasking—"

"Switchtasking!" Helen corrected.

"Of course—switchtasking." Phil grinned. "When your family understands that you are going to be focused and pay attention to them in the moment, they will feel greater respect toward you. They will trust you more. It's a process that takes time, but it will make a difference."

Helen sighed in satisfaction and plopped down into her chair. "All I know is that I felt wonderful. It's the first time in years that I've been that . . . present . . . with my family." She paused. "You know, I'm amazed I hadn't been aware that I was switchtasking on them. I think most people do it to each other all the time, and they don't even realize it!"

Phil nodded. "That is a big part of why multitasking is worse than a lie. When we act as if multitasking is a good thing, we seriously damage our relationships with others. It's not just about families. It's about coworkers. It's about friends. It's about the cashier at the store who is a real person but we're treating them like one task among many to be performed. This damage to relationships that occurs over time is one more part of the switching cost of switchtasking."

> *A female patient asked me if I thought it was abnormal that her husband lays the BlackBerry on the bed when they make love.*
>
> —Dr. Edward Hallowell, expert on attention deficit disorder in an interview with *USA TODAY*

Helen became very thoughtful. "Phil, have you ever thought about what switchtasking costs a company in terms of sales?"

Phil raised his eyebrows in surprise. "Sales? What do you mean?"

Helen smiled, clearly pleased that she had thought of something Phil had not. "Well, if my employees switchtask when dealing with customers, that's got to hurt customer satisfaction. Even if this happens just a bit at a time, customers are going to start to get the feeling we don't care."

"Interesting," Phil said. "Go on."

> *If you chase two rabbits, you will not catch either one.*
>
> —Russian proverb

"Well, if customers feel that we don't care, sooner or later they are going to take their business to someplace that does," Helen continued. "Plus, if you just think about the sales process itself, it can have an impact. If our sales reps switchtask while dealing with retail store owners, it will start costing us over time."

Phil pulled out a notepad. "Do you mind if I write that down?"

Helen laughed, "Does that mean I get to charge you for this meeting?"

"No comment," Phil replied dryly.

THE STEPS

"Okay, so now that you've taught me something this morning," Phil continued, "what can I teach you? What questions do you have?"

Helen dove in with enthusiasm. "Well, you've thoroughly convinced me that multitasking is a lie. I'm a believer. But how do I stop it? Everyone else around me is still going crazy and won't slow down."

"I can help you with that," Phil replied. "Let's start by writing down what you know you can do so far. Can we use that whiteboard on the wall?"

"Be my guest," Helen bowed and gestured graciously.

Phil stood up from the desk and walked over to the whiteboard. "You start, Helen. Let's review what you know so far. What steps can you take to stop switchtasking?"

Phil wrote down each of Helen's bullet points as she reviewed their previous day's discussion out loud. When she was finished, Phil had written the following on the whiteboard:

- Recognize that multitasking is a lie.
- Understand the difference between background tasking and switchtasking.
- Become aware of the truth about how you have been using your time on a weekly basis.
- Create a new and realistic budget for how you will use your time on a weekly basis.
- Schedule recurring appointments with your key people.
- Set expectations, and create personal "shop hours" to let people know when you will be available.

"That's a great start," Phil said.

"I can see how just making those few things happen will make a big difference," Helen added. "What else can I do to stop switchtasking?"

"Here are some other suggestions that my clients have found helpful." Phil wrote a few more bullet points on the board:

- Resist making active switches.
- Minimize all passive switches.
- Give people your full attention when dealing with them.
- Schedule plenty of travel time between appointments.
- Never commit to something without your calendar in hand.

Phil turned from the board to face Helen. "What questions do you have about these?"

"Can you refresh my mind on what you mean about active and passive switches?" Helen asked.

"Active switches are the ones that you choose to make. Remember yesterday when we discussed a typical hour in your day? Any time you were the one initiating the switch, you were making an active switch," Phil

> *And now, excuse me while I interrupt myself.*
>
> —Murray Walker, motor sports commentator

89

explained. "Remind yourself to hold off switching from one thing to another whenever you are in control of your schedule."

"Right," Helen said. "Basically I need to be in control of myself. I need to slow down the need for constant switches."

"You've got it," Phil nodded. "Now, regarding passive switches, those are the ones that come at you without your immediate choice. You can minimize these by doing things such as turning off the computer alerts for new e-mail."

"What about instant messaging or phone texting? My kids use those things all the time," Helen groaned.

Phil laughed. "By not using instant messaging programs, you'll find that your passive interruptions will drop drastically. I recommend that unless you're trying to communicate with a teenager, instant messaging is usually an inefficient business tool. Of course, there are exceptions to that guideline, but I don't think your business fits any of those rare exceptions."

"Wow." Helen's eyes widened. "We need to have a company discussion about that one. I'll bet half my managers are instant messaging all day long."

"And probably more than half of those messages have little to do with business," Phil added. "Combine the loss of just plain work time with the switching costs of each interruption, and it's easy to see why your employees on average are losing 28 percent of their workday."

"What would you suggest we use to replace instant messaging?" Helen asked.

6.5

Average hours per day of media exposure for kids aged 8 to 18.

8.5

Total hours per day of media exposure for those same kids due to media multitasking.

—Kaiser Family Foundation Survey

"Great question," Phil said. "Instant messaging is in your face. It is a very potent passive interruption that forces its attention on you. Because of that, my clients have found that restricting company communication to active interruption methods, such as voice mail or e-mail, works well in most situations.

"However," Phil continued, "if you absolutely need to use instant messaging, make sure that your company uses a program with a 'Do Not Disturb' feature, so that passive interruptions can't get through."

62.4

Percentage of people surveyed who feel it is acceptable to interrupt work to answer a personal question from a friend.

—Basex Research study

Helen wrote herself a note. "I'll get on that immediately."

Phil let her finish and then said, "May I add a little caution to taking action to curtail switchtasking in your company?"

"What is it?"

"Well, keep in mind that you and I have had a long discussion and training on the ills of switchtasking." Phil leaned forward in his chair a bit. "Do you think your managers understand passive interruptions and switchtasking?"

Helen jerked her head back in surprise. "Oh. I see. They still think switchtasking—multitasking—is good, don't they?"

"Exactly," Phil said. "Until they understand that the multitasking they've prided themselves on for so long is actually hurting them and the company, they will resist any change you make away from it. Remember how Sally resisted the idea at first?" Phil leaned back and put his hands together in a moment of contemplation. "It's not their fault, really. They've been taught for so long that multitasking is good. They've come to pride themselves on it."

"I know I sure did," Helen interjected.

"Right," Phil nodded. "Consider how your perspective changed over the last two days. What did it take for you to recognize that multitasking was worse than a lie?"

Slow and steady wins the race.

—Tortoise to the Hare, attributed to Aesop

Helen looked up to the ceiling in thought. "I guess it was the process you took me through. I had to see the truth, step by step."

"You've got it," Phil said. "Remember that helping people understand the simple truth will help them change their behavior faster than simply trying to get them to change their behavior." Phil smiled. "What if I had come in yesterday and told you that you needed to spend more time with your family? What if I had told you that you needed to focus more when talking to people?"

Helen laughed loudly. "I probably would have told you where to go and how to get there!"

Phil nodded. "Then how can you expect anything different from your managers?"

THE SYSTEMS

Helen rested her hand on her chin. After a long pause, she said, "Can you help me with this? I'd rather have you than me talk to them."

"What did you have in mind?" Phil asked.

"I guess I'm wondering if there is a way you can teach this to a group," Helen said. "Is that something you can do?"

"I'd be glad to help you." Phil reached for his briefcase. "Let me pull out my calendar."

"Right." Helen pointed toward the whiteboard. "Never commit to something without your calendar in hand." She looked around the room as if searching for something. "What if I have a calendar, but I'm not using it as well as I should?"

Technology provides the very tools that are supposed to make us more productive, but we haven't done a very good job of deploying them, training users to use them, or training managers on how to manage those who use them.

—Jonathan B. Spira, CEO and chief analyst, Basex Research

Phil grinned. "Then you're probably like most people I talk to. Most people have excellent tools. They spend a lot of money on planners, electronic planners, special phones, and the latest gadget. Yet few know how to use them properly, and of the few who do, even fewer use them as much as they should."

Phil opened his calendar and pulled out a pen. "Before we schedule a training session with your managers as a group, may I make a recommendation?"

"Please do."

"There really are two major steps to getting your business as a whole off switchtasking dependency. One of them you've already suggested: we can educate your people on the ills of multitasking. The other is that we can make some improvements to how the company as a whole operates. In other words, you're going to make some changes to the systems of the business."

Phil grabbed his notebook and started drawing.

BUSINESS SYSTEMS

PERSONAL SYSTEMS

Helen tilted her head to the side. "By business systems, you mean our processes, right? The way we do things here? The way we manufacture, communicate with each other, and so on?"

Phil gave Helen a thumbs-up. "You've got it. Based on your understanding, why are systems important for your business?"

"Well," Helen said thoughtfully, "the main reason is that without those business systems, people will just do things any way that they want to. Everything will become chaos. We won't be consistent in dealing with our customers."

"Exactly right," Phil nodded. "Let's keep that thought and continue. Perhaps more important than improving business systems is to help you, the leader of this company, get your own personal systems in order." He began writing on his notepad again.

"Personal systems?" Helen asked. "What do you mean?"

"Your personal systems are the way you operate as a person: how you handle e-mail, voice mail, faxes, the ideas in your head, your work space organization, how you use your calendar, and so on. If you don't have clear, solid personal systems in place for yourself, what happens?"

Helen let air rush out in a big sigh. "What happens is what has been happening to me. I'm at the mercy of everyone and everything else." After thinking for a moment, she added, "It's the same as with my business. Without systems, I become inconsistent."

Phil added more to the drawing:

**BUSINESS
SYSTEMS**
(THE COMPANY)

**PERSONAL
SYSTEMS**
(YOU)

He continued, "As I walked down the hall to your office yesterday and today, I saw managers and employees rushing around. The culture of stress and tension was palpable." After a pause, Phil added, "I saw a business that reflects its leader."

Helen sighed. "As much as I hate to admit it, you're right, but we've been aware of it. We've done everything we can to change our culture. We've added fun things to the break room. We have more company parties." Helen shrugged. "What am I missing?"

"Those are all great things." Phil nodded approvingly. "I'm sure they did have a great impact. All that aside, I'm not sure you caught what I said."

"What do you mean?" Helen looked a bit defensive.

"Your company is reflecting you." Phil gave her a moment to let that sink in, then began scribbling on the notepad again. "Let me show this to you in a different way."

Helen stared at the drawing for close to a full minute. Slowly the understanding grew on her face. "You mean my personal systems have an impact on the business systems? My way of doing things will affect the company's way of doing things?"

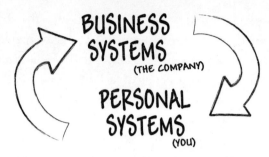

"Right." Phil tapped the table for emphasis. "If we want to change this company, then where is the best place to start?"

"Me?" Helen asked.

"You've got it," Phil nodded. "I started with you by talking about multitasking because it's such a familiar topic. Multitasking is an easy place for anyone to start making positive change. Yet it's just one of many areas where we need to build your personal systems. For instance, how you use your calendar is another important component."

Helen appeared to be mulling over the idea. "So what do you recommend?"

"Before we start training your employees, let's finish the job we started," Phil said. "What you've learned about switchtasking has already had an impact on you personally. It's had an impact on your family."

Helen continued Phil's thought without missing a beat. "It's going to have an impact on my business. People are going to see that I've changed the way I operate. I'm going to protect my time and minimize interruptions." She began thinking out loud to herself now. "They are going to learn to hold off most of their questions until our recurring meetings. They will see that I'm focused and pay attention to them. They will see that I'm not switchtasking as much as I used to. Hopefully, my management team will recognize the change and start to follow my example."

> *Dress me slowly, for I am in a great rush.*
>
> —Napoleon Bonaparte, reportedly to his manservant before a great battle

"Yes. Over time they will," Phil assured her. "Later on we can give them training that will help them change their own personal systems."

Helen jumped in. "Because by changing the manager, we'll change their division, won't we? Isn't each division a reflection of its management?"

Phil nodded approvingly. "You've taught me again, Helen." He jotted down a note to himself. Phil paused, then grabbed his calendar. "Are you ready to finish the job we started? Are you ready to build your personal systems?"

"Yes. I'm ready," Helen said.

Phil grinned. "Pull out your calendar. You and I need to set up *our* recurring meetings."

THE FOLLOW–UP

The room filled with brief applause as Phil stepped away from the podium. Helen was sitting in the front row of the conference room talking excitedly to several of her GreenGarb employees.

Phil reflected back on what had happened in the three months since his first meeting with Helen. First, he began meeting with Helen regularly. He had first helped her build her personal systems and establish a new time budget. Then he had helped Helen set up recurring meetings with her employees—starting with Sally, of course.

At first, the employees didn't know what to think. They had been so used to being half-ignored by Helen and the other managers for a long time.

Gradually, though, they realized that Helen wasn't using a technique on them, and she wasn't going through a seminar zealot phase. She was simply listening to them, giving them time, and focusing on the moment.

After Helen mastered her personal systems, she and Phil had agreed that the time was right to begin training management. He worked with them as a team and individually to help them follow the example Helen had set. The gains in both productivity and job satisfaction were measurable and growing daily.

A familiar face approached Phil. She was holding Phil's coat folded neatly over one arm. "It hope you don't mind if I gathered your coat up for you. I think you'll need it. It's raining something fierce outside."

"Thank you very much, Sally," Phil said warmly. "I appreciate your looking out for me."

"Don't mention it."

As he put each arm into his jacket, Phil said, "You know, we need to set up a time to follow up on our little wager. I think you owe me some cookies."

Sally laughed. "Not so fast! Helen's better, I'll give you that, but let's just hope it lasts!"

"I wouldn't expect anything less from you, Sally," Phil said, picking up his briefcase. "If you feel that Helen's change hasn't lived up to your expectations, there's still a nice filet mignon waiting for you and a friend."

"We'll see. We'll see," Sally said, waving as she turned to speak with a colleague.

It took Phil a while to extricate himself from the room as he shook hands and exchanged kind words with well-wishers, but finally he walked briskly through the hallway to the building entrance. As he looked through the glass doors, he realized he would have to make a run through what was now an intense downpour.

He swung open the doors and made a dash for his car. Feeling into the pocket of his coat for his keys, he pushed the automatic lock on his sedan. It chirped and flashed its lights at him through the storm. He threw open the door and tossed his briefcase over to the passenger seat. He began to swing himself quickly into the driver's side when he noticed something on his seat wrapped in colorful cellophane.

Phil laughed as he picked up the plate, sat down and closed the door behind him. Carefully he removed the attached note and began to read:

Phil–
I haven't had to wait in line for Helen for over a month.
Sally
P.S. These are from the grocery store. I told you it was dangerous to trust me to cook.

Phil set the cookies in the passenger seat, smiled to himself, and turned the key in the ignition.

WORKSHEETS

SWITCHTASKING EXERCISE

Result

The following exercise will help you quickly understand the negative impact of switchtasking on
efficiency.

Steps

First Pass
1. Have the worksheet on page (111) ready.
2. Have a timer with a second hand ready. For best
   results, have another person time you.
3. In the first row of the worksheet, recopy the
   phrase, "Multitasking is worse than a lie."
   However, for every letter you write in the M row,
   switch to the second row (labeled 1) and write
   the corresponding number. If you complete this
   correctly, you will have the phrase "Multitasking
   is worse than a lie" written in the first row, and
   the numbers 1 to 27 in the second row. (See
   page 41 for an example.)

4. Ready, set, go!

5. After you have completed the last number, 27, write down your total time to completion at the end of the second row.

Second Pass

1. Have the timer ready again. For best results, have another person time you.

2. In the third row, recopy the phrase, "Multitasking is worse than a lie." After copying the entire phrase in the third row, switch to the fourth row and write the numbers 1 to 27. If you complete this correctly, you will have the phrase "Multitasking is worse than a lie" written in the third row and the numbers 1 to 27 in the fourth row. (See page 43 for an example.)

3. Ready, set, go!

4. Compare the time to completion between the second and fourth rows. Typically a person takes twice as long to complete this exercise when switchtasking (first pass) versus focusing on one task at a time (second pass).

Multitasking is worse than a lie

M

1

M

1

REPORTS WORKSHEET

Result

By holding recurring meetings with people who contact you frequently, you'll greatly reduce the number of passive interruptions in your life.

This worksheet will help you determine which of your relationships will benefit the most from recurring meetings.

Steps

1. In the Work Relationship column of the Professional Reports Worksheet on pages 116–117, write the name of each person you have contact with on a *regular* basis. "Regular" means that you talk with them for work purposes at least once per month.
2. In the Comments column, write any comments that you feel would be helpful to keep in mind about this relationship—for example, personality characteristics, the typical items discussed, or position title.
3. In the first Needs column under Manage? write a score of 3 for this person if your job requires you

to manage this person or if this person is directly accountable to you for his or her success. If not, score 0.

4. In the next column, Questions? score this person as to how often he or she asks you questions. Write a 0, 1, 2, or 3 using the following scale:

0 = Never
1 = Rarely
2 = Occasionally
3 = Frequently

5. Complete the remaining columns using the same scale you did for Manage?
   - *Calendar?* How often do you need to coordinate calendars?
   - *Delegate?* How often do you delegate items to them?
   - *Coordinate?* How often do the two of you need to coordinate your efforts to achieve successful results?
   - *Assist?* How often does this individual personally assist you in your work?
   - *Follow Up?* How often do you need to follow up with this person to ensure his or her success?

6. In the Needs Score column, add up the scores for that person from all the Needs columns, and write the result.

7. After you have completed the previous steps for every person in the relationships column, use the Rank column to rank them according to their Needs scores. For instance, if you have listed five people in the Work Relationship column, and John had the highest score, then rank John as 1. If Vera had the lowest score, rank her as 5, and so on for all ranks in between.

8. Proceed to the Personal Reports Worksheet.

9. In the Personal Relationship column, write the names of each person outside your worklife you have contact with on a regular basis—for example, your spouse, children, close friends, and contacts in church or community service.

10. Add any helpful notes to the Comments column.

11. In the first Needs column under Advisor? write a score of 3 for this person if you have an established mentor, spouse, leader, or parent relationship with this person. If not, score 0.

12. Repeat steps 4 to 7 as described in the Professional Reports Worksheet section.

PROFESSIONAL REPORTS WORKSHEET

Work Relationship	Comments	Advisor?
Write name here	Write comments if helpful	0 or 3

NEEDS							
Questions?	Calendar?	Delegate?	Coordinate?	Assist?	Follow up?	NEEDS SCORE	RANK
0–3	0–3	0–3	0–3	0–3	0–3	Add up	Highest = #1

PERSONAL REPORTS WORKSHEET		
Personal Relationship	Comments	Advisor?
Write name here	Write comments if helpful	0 or 3

| NEEDS | | | | | | | |
Questions?	Calendar?	Delegate?	Coordinate?	Assist?	Follow up?	NEEDS SCORE	RANK
0–3	0–3	0–3	0–3	0–3	0–3	Add up	Highest = #1

RECURRING MEETINGS WORKSHEET

Result

You've already completed the Reports Worksheets and have a better understanding of the needs of those you work with and spend time with. The Recurring Meetings Worksheet will help you find a starting point in determining how often you should meet.

At the end of this worksheet, you will also have a clear action plan and commitment to begin holding recurring meetings.

Note: Over time, you will find you need to adjust your recurring meeting schedule. This worksheet is a starting point only.

Steps

1. Starting with the highest-ranked professional relationship from the Professional Reports Worksheet, transfer the Rank, Needs Score, and name of each relationship to the Recurring Meetings Worksheet provided on pages 124–125.

2. Now use the Frequency column to indicate how often you plan on meeting with this person. Here are some rules of thumb:

- Dedicated personal assistants almost always need to meet with you daily.
- Most relationships with a Needs Score higher than 18 likely need to have a recurring meeting with you once a day.
- Relationships with Needs Scores from 14 to 17 likely need to meet with you weekly.
- Most relationships, meaning Needs Scores from 6 to 13, will benefit the most from a semi-monthly meeting, such as "every other week," "first and third weeks of the month," or "second and fourth weeks of month."
- Relationships with Needs Scores less than 6 likely need a meeting only once a month or possibly no recurring meeting.

3. Determine the length of each meeting. Use the following rules of thumb:

- The higher the frequency, the shorter the meeting. In other words, when you meet with someone daily, the meetings should be kept to 15 minutes. If you meet with someone monthly, typically 1 hour is appropriate.

- Avoid recurring meetings for less than 15 minutes because they are likely to get pushed off or ignored.
- Avoid recurring meetings longer than 60 minutes because they are likely to provide an opportunity to waste time.

4. Get together with the person for the purpose of setting up your recurring meetings.

5. Together, determine the best day and time for the meetings. In general, schedule recurring meetings for when neither of you is likely to be interrupted.

6. Make sure that each of you has scheduled the appointment in your calendar by placing a check mark in the appropriate columns of the worksheet.

7. Repeat these steps for the relationships from your Personal Reports Worksheet.

RECURRING MEETINGS WORKSHEET

RANK	NEEDS SCORE	Name	Frequency
			☐ Daily ☐ Weekly ☐ Every other week ☐ 1st and 3rd weeks of month ☐ 2nd and 4th weeks of month ☐ Monthly (Date_____)
			☐ Daily ☐ Weekly ☐ Every other week ☐ 1st and 3rd weeks of month ☐ 2nd and 4th weeks of month ☐ Monthly (Date_____)
			☐ Daily ☐ Weekly ☐ Every other week ☐ 1st and 3rd weeks of month ☐ 2nd and 4th weeks of month ☐ Monthly (Date_____)
			☐ Daily ☐ Weekly ☐ Every other week ☐ 1st and 3rd weeks of month ☐ 2nd and 4th weeks of month ☐ Monthly (Date_____)

Length	Day	Time	Location	You Calendared	They Calendared
☐ 15 min ☐ 30 min ☐ 60 min ☐ _____	☐ Every Weekday ☐ Monday ☐ Tuesday ☐ Wednesday ☐ Thursday ☐ Friday ☐ Saturday ☐ Sunday	to			
☐ 15 min ☐ 30 min ☐ 60 min ☐ _____	☐ Every Weekday ☐ Monday ☐ Tuesday ☐ Wednesday ☐ Thursday ☐ Friday ☐ Saturday ☐ Sunday	to			
☐ 15 min ☐ 30 min ☐ 60 min ☐ _____	☐ Every Weekday ☐ Monday ☐ Tuesday ☐ Wednesday ☐ Thursday ☐ Friday ☐ Saturday ☐ Sunday	to			
☐ 15 min ☐ 30 min ☐ 60 min ☐ _____	☐ Every Weekday ☐ Monday ☐ Tuesday ☐ Wednesday ☐ Thursday ☐ Friday ☐ Saturday ☐ Sunday	to			

TRUTH OF TIME WORKSHEET

Result

This worksheet will help you understand how you have been using all of the 168 hours you have in an average week. By understanding the truth of how you have been using your time, you'll see where you want to make changes in how you use your time, if any.

After you assess how you use your time, you'll be able to create a new budget for how you want to allocate your time in the future.

Steps

1. Using the worksheet on pages 130–131, add in the Activity column activities you perform in your life as a whole—for example, "Family Time," "Hobby," "Exercise," "Housework," "Spiritual," "Community Service," and so on. Use categories that are broad enough so that you do not need to use more than the rows provided.

2. In the Boundary column, define what each activity means. The purpose of doing this is to make sure that each activity is accounted for and there is no chance of overlapping how you account for time. For instance, suppose that you list both Family Time and Spouse Time separately in the Activity column. In the Boundary column, clarify the difference between the two, such as saying that "time alone with spouse" applies only to Spouse Time but that time spent with both spouse and children should be counted as part of the Family Time activity.

3. In the Current column, estimate how many hours in an average week you spend in each activity. Round to the nearest half-hour. Notice that the Lost activity already has "7" filled in. This is because, in general, each person unavoidably loses an hour a day due to the accumulation of small, random activities such as getting up from the chair, getting a snack, and so on. Pay attention to differences in your weekend schedule in doing your estimates. For instance, if you sleep an average of 7 hours every night but get an extra hour of sleep on Friday and Saturday nights, then the total for the Sleep row would be 51, not 49.

Important: Do *not* try to reconcile the total to 168 as you go. Just make your best guess. In the next step you'll have a chance to clean things up.

4. Total up all your estimates in the Current column, and then subtract from 168 (the number of hours in a week). You will likely end up with a number such as +4 or −7.5. (If you estimated exactly 168, then skip to step 6.)

5. Now, since there is only one time line and only one you, you need to bring your time estimates back into balance. Clean up your estimates by adding or subtracting time from different activities until your total reaches 168. These are the typical culprits for making errors in your time estimates:

   • Not clearly defining activities in the Boundary column, causing overlap between one or more activities.

   • Over- or underestimating the largest blocks of time, such as sleep or work.

   • Forgetting an activity and failing to account for it.

   • Not accounting for switchtasking in your estimates. To correct this, you need to be more specific in your Boundary definition.

ACTIVITY	BOUNDARY
Lost Time	Scratching nose, getting up from a chair, and so on
Sleep	Total hours of actual sleep, including daytime naps
Prep	Showering, dressing, and so on, morning and night
Work	Primary job work-related activities, including travel to and from office
Personal Recreation	

CURRENT	FUTURE
7	7

6. Now that you understand how you are using your time, look for and highlight the rows that you want to change.

7. Move to the Future column. Choose a date at some point in the future (usually about a month from now works well). Next, create a new time budget according to how you want your use of time to look by the date that you decided on.

8. Recheck the numbers, and make sure they total to 168, just as you did in steps 4 and 5.

9. Locate a blank weekly calendar that shows the hours. Map out how you want to budget your time, using a different highlighter color for each type of activity.

SOURCES

González, V., and Mark, G. "Constant, Constant, Multi-Tasking Craziness: Managing Multiple Working Spheres." Paper presented at Conference on Human Factors in Computing Systems 2004, Vienna, Austria, Apr. 24–29.

González, V., and Mark, G. "Managing Currents of Work: Multi-Tasking Among Multiple Collaborations." Paper presented at the Proceedings of the Ninth European Conference on Computer-Supported Cooperative Work, Paris, Sept. 18–22, 2005.

Harvard Business Essentials, *Time Management: Increase Your Personal Productivity and Effectiveness.* Boston: Harvard Business School Press, 2005.

Hallowell, E. M. "Overloaded Circuits: Why Smart People Underperform." *Harvard Business Review,* 2005, *83*(1), 54–62.

Mark, G., González, V., and Harris, J. "No Task Left Behind? Examining the Nature of Fragmented Work." Paper presented at Conference on Human Factors in Computing Systems, Portland, Ore., April 2–7, 2005.

Meyer, D. E. Interview by Stephen Frazier. *CNN Tonight,* Aug. 5, 2001.

Moran, M. "Researchers Find Neural Bottleneck' Thwarts Multitasking." *Vanderbilt Register,* Jan. 22, 2007. Accessed Jan. 11, 2008, at http://www.vanderbilt.edu/register/articles?id=31525.

"Multitasking." UrbanDictionary.com. Accessed Apr. 12, 2007, at http://www.urbandictionary.com/define.php?term=multitasking&r=f.

"Multitasking." Webopedia.com. Accessed Aug. 3, 2007, at http:// itmanagement.webopedia.com/TERM/M/multitasking .html.

"Multitasking." Wikipedia.com. Accessed Aug. 2, 2007, at http://en.wikipedia.org/wiki/Multitasking.

Puente, M. "Blackberry Blackout?" *USA Today,* Feb. 1, 2006. Accessed Jan. 11, 2008, at http://www.usatoday.com/tech/products/services/2006-02-01-blackberry-life_x.htm.

Richtel, M. "The Lure of Data: Is It Addictive?" *New York Times,* July 6, 2003.

Roberts, D. F., Foehr, U. G., and Rideout, V. *Generation M: Media in the Lives of 8–18 Year-Olds.* Menlo Park, Calif.: 2005.

Rosen, M. "The Perils of Multitasking." *Scholastic Parents,* Feb. 28, 2007. Accessed Jan. 11, 2008, at http://www2 .scholastic.com/browse/article.jsp?id=11595.

Shellenbarger, S. "Juggling Too Many Tasks Could Make You Stupid." *Career Journal.com,* Feb. 28, 2003. Accessed May 5, 2007, at http://www.careerjournal.com/columnists/ workfamily/20030228-workfamily.html.

Shellenbarger, S. "Who's the Better Multitasker? Female Rats Provide Clues." *Career Journal.com,* Mar. 21, 2003. Accessed Apr. 15, 2007, at http://www.careerjournal.com/ columnists/workfamily/20030321-workfamily.html.

Spira, J. B., and Feintuch, J. B. *The Cost of Not Paying Attention: How Interruptions Impact Knowledge Worker Productivity.* New York: Basex, 2005.

Strang, A. L., González, V. M., and Mark, G. *Excuse Me: Interrupting Working Spheres.* Irvine: University of California, 2004.

Strayer, D. L., Drews, F. A., and Crouch, D. J. "A Comparison of the Cell Phone Driver and the Drunk Driver." *Human Factors,* 2006, *48*(2), 381–391.

Wallis, C. C. "The Multitasking Generation." *Time,* Mar. 19, 2006.

Wallis, C. C., and Steptoe, S. "Help! I've Lost My Focus." *Time,* Jan. 8, 2006.

Wallis, C. C., and Steptoe, S. "The Case for Doing One Thing at a Time." *Time,* Jan. 8, 2006.

THE AUTHOR

Dave Crenshaw was born in southern California and grew up in the shadow of Utah's Rocky Mountains. He began his business coaching career in 1998 by becoming the youngest independent consultant for one of the world's largest small business coaching firms. He had already coached business owners several times his age before receiving his B.S. in business management-entrepreneurship. Dave is the creator of the Fresh Juice Strategy program, a system of helping business owners and managers get the most out of themselves and their businesses. He has coached and consulted business owners and managers from London to Manila and from San Francisco to New York. He resides in Utah with his wife, Katherine, and loves playing football with his son, Stratton.

For more information about Dave Crenshaw and Fresh Juice Strategy, please visit his Web site at www.davecrenshaw.com.